W9-CFA-418

BEAUTIFUL BIRDS
of
HAWAI'I
COLORING BOOK

Written and Illustrated
by
Patrick Ching

3565 Harding Ave. Honolulu, HI 96816
(808) 734-7159   www.besspress.com

BEAUTIFUL BIRDS OF HAWAI'I is a coloring book featuring an assortment of rare as well as commonly seen birds.

At the upper left corner of each information page is the word "Endemic," "Indigenous," "Migratory," or "Introduced." Endemic and **indigenous** birds arrived in Hawai'i on their own power. They are considered **native** to Hawai'i. **Indigenous** birds are those that are native to Hawai'i and also exist in other parts of the world. **Endemic** birds are those that are found only in Hawai'i. **Migratory** birds usually spend the winter in Hawai'i and fly far away to their breeding grounds in the summer. **Introduced** birds were brought to Hawai'i by man. Most of the birds we see in the lowlands were introduced to Hawai'i from other parts of the world.

At the upper right corner of the information page may be the word "Threatened," "Endangered," or "Extinct." Threatened birds are those that are becoming rare, and **endangered** birds are especially low in number. **Extinct** birds have died out completely and are gone forever. More birds have become extinct in Hawai'i than in all the rest of the United States put together.

COLORING: Color crayons or colored pencils are recommended for coloring this book. For accurate coloring, use the small pictures on the back of this book as a guide.

NĒNĒ
(Hawaiian Goose)

Hawai'i's state bird is a goose called the nēnē. Though nēnē do enjoy water, their feet have less webbing than the feet of other geese. This allows them to survive better on rocky terrain with scattered vegetation.

The nēnē's diet includes seeds, grasses and fruits. The native 'ōhelo berry is among its favorite foods.

In the late 1950s the nēnē population was nearly extinct. Through the efforts of captive breeding programs, the nēnē's numbers increased and hundreds of birds were reintroduced into the wild. Today the nēnē can be found on the islands of Hawai'i, Maui, and Kaua'i. They can also be seen at the Honolulu Zoo on O'ahu.

The plant pictured next to the nēnē is the silversword, which grows on the upper volcanic slopes of Maui and Hawai'i.

Patrick Ching '85 ©

RED-CRESTED CARDINAL

This cardinal can be found in the lowland areas of Oʻahu, Kauaʻi, Molokaʻi, Lānaʻi, and Maui. It was brought to Hawaiʻi from South America around 1930. The adult birds have bright-red heads, while younger birds have rust-colored heads. These birds often travel in pairs or family groups and are common in parks and on lawns.

NORTHERN CARDINAL

Also known as the Kentucky cardinal or red cardinal, this bird can be found on all the main islands. It was brought to Hawaiʻi from the eastern United States in 1929. Male birds are bright red with a distinctive black patch around their bills. Female birds are more brown in color than the males and lack the black patch around their bills. Cardinals have a loud, melodious song that can be heard from far away. They are especially vocal in the morning hours.

RED-CRESTED CARDINAL

NORTHERN CARDINAL

Patrick Ching '92©

'ALAE 'ULA
(Hawaiian Gallinule)

'Alae 'ula live in the wetlands of O'ahu and Kaua'i. They are no longer found on Maui, Moloka'i, or the Big Island. Some of the best places to see them are in wetland taro patches, where they nest and feed on snails and plants.

According to legend, long ago a gallinule flew up to the heavens and stole a stick of fire from the gods. He brought the fire back down to earth as a gift to the Hawaiian people. In the process, the bird's forehead was scorched by the fire, and today the descendants of that brave bird proudly wear the red and yellow mark of the flame.

Patrick Ching 92

MŌLĪ

(Laysan Albatross)

With a wingspan of nearly seven feet, the mōlī glides through the air. These birds spend most of their lives at sea and during the nonbreeding season remain at sea for months at a time. The favorite food of the mōlī is squid. During the breeding season (November to August) the birds return to their main breeding grounds in the Northwest Hawaiian Islands. Recently, more and more albatross have been nesting on the main Hawaiian islands and especially on Kauaʻi.

The mating dance of the mōlī is really fun to watch. The birds whistle, moan, and clap their beaks as they bob up and down and shake their heads. On land the mōlī seem very awkward and are often called "gooney birds."

Patrick Ching '92

'APAPANE

The 'apapane lives in the upper rainforests of all the main Hawaiian Islands. Its bright-red feathers match the color of the nectar of lehua blossoms, which is one of this bird's favorite foods. Feather collectors in ancient times caught the 'apapane by putting sticky tree sap on the branches next to the blossoming lehua. When the bird landed on the sticky branch, it was caught and its feathers collected.

'ĀKOHEKOHE

(Crested Honeycreeper)

High on the slopes of Haleakalā volcano, on the island of Maui, lives the 'ākohekohe. It once lived on Moloka'i, but is now believed to be extinct on that island. The 'ākohekohe feeds mostly on lehua nectar, but also eats worms and insects. It is an aggressive bird that will often chase other birds away from its favorite lehua blossoms.

'APAPANE

'ĀKOHEKOHE

Patrick Ching '92

RING-NECKED PHEASANT

This introduced game bird lives in grassy fields and dry forests of all the main islands. It will often freeze when approached and hide itself in the grass. If you get too close it will suddenly cry out and burst into flight.

The male is very colorful, with a dark green head, white ring around the neck, red wattles on its face, and long tail feathers. The female is rather dull in comparison.

'ELEPAIO

One of Hawai'i's more common native forest birds is the 'elepaio. The 'elepaio can be found on O'ahu, Kaua'i, and the Big Island. It is a curious bird that often approaches hikers and follows them through the forest.

Hawaiians believed that the 'elepaio was the friendly guardian of the canoe builders. When choosing a koa tree to build into a canoe, the canoe builders would watch the 'elepaio. If the bird pecked at the desired tree, it meant that the tree was infested with bugs and worms and was not good to use. If the 'elepaio landed on the tree and flew off without pecking at it, then the tree was harvested and hollowed out into a canoe.

Patrick Ching '86 ©

KOAʻE ʻULA
(Red-Tailed Tropicbird)

A bright-red bill and streamerlike tail feathers make the red-tailed tropicbird easy to spot. During their breeding season, from March to October, groups of these birds can be seen flying in backward circles and calling to one another. They are especially active during midday. Red-tailed tropicbirds nest on the ground under shrubs on the remote Northwest Hawaiian Islands. The best place to see them in the main islands is at the Kīlauea Point Wildlife Refuge on Kauaʻi, where they nest in the holes in the cliffs overlooking the sea.

Indigenous

KOAʻE KEA
(White-Tailed Tropicbird)

The white-tailed tropicbird can often be seen soaring over coastal inland valleys and waterfalls. Like the red-tailed tropicbird, it feeds on fish and squid, which it gets by plunging into the ocean. White-tailed tropicbirds are slightly smaller than the red-tails, though their tail feathers are noticeably longer. The tail feathers of both tropicbird species were used by the Hawaiians to make headdresses and feathered standards called kāhili.

KOAʻE ʻULA

KOAʻE KEA

Patrick Ching '92

COMMON MYNAH

Common on all main islands, the mynah is one of the best-known birds in Hawai'i. It was brought to Hawai'i from India in 1865.

   With their distinctive brown and yellow coloring and loud, raspy calls, these birds are easy to notice. During the day they usually travel in pairs, but in the late afternoon they gather in large flocks to roost in trees. The noise made by the flocking mynahs can be deafening at times, and in some cases the mynahs become major pests.

Patrik Ching '92©

'ALALĀ
(Hawaiian Crow)

When Captain Cook arrived in Hawai'i, he noted that the native crow was abundant and respected by the Hawaiians. Some even kept crows tethered as pets. Today the crows are on the brink of extinction. The only wild population is on the island of Hawai'i, where only about a dozen birds are known to exist. Breeding the crows in captivity is a slow and difficult task.

In Hawaiian, "'alalā" means "to cry out loud." Indeed, today's Hawaiian crows have something very serious to cry about.

Patrick Ching '92 ©

ʻŪLILI
(Wandering Tattler)

This playful shorebird is a seasonal visitor to Hawaiʻi. In the winter months from August through April, it can be seen on all the Hawaiian islands as it cruises the shoreline and mud flats in search of food. Its meals consist mostly of mollusks and other small invertebrates.

In April the ʻūlili is usually seen alone or in pairs. Its gray body and yellow legs make it easy to recognize.

According to Hawaiian lore, the ʻūlili played the role of a messenger or sometimes even a spy.

Patrick Ching '9?

PUEO
(Hawaiian Short-Eared Owl)

Owls have long been a symbol of wisdom and spirituality throughout the world. The same is true for the Hawaiian owl, which is regarded as an 'aumakua, or guardian spirit, by many Hawaiians.

The Hawaiian owl, or pueo, can be seen soaring over the grasslands and cliffs of all the main Hawaiian islands. It usually hunts in the daytime for rodents, insects, and sometimes birds.

The pueo is often confused with the introduced barn owl, which was brought to Hawai'i in 1958 to eat rats and mice. The barn owl is larger than the pueo and has a distinctive heart-shaped face.

BARN OWL

Patrick Ching '85 ©

COMMON PEAFOWL

Wild peafowl are most common on the islands of Hawai'i, Maui, and O'ahu. Male birds, called "peacocks," have long blue and green tails, which they present in a fanlike display to attract females. The Hawaiian name for peacock is "pīkake." Peacocks are most vocal in the evenings, when they roost in trees. Their loud calls can be heard for great distances.

Patrick Ching '92©

ʻŌʻŌ
(Hawaiian Honeyeater)

Several species of ʻōʻō existed in Hawaiʻi. The Big Island, Oʻahu, and Molokaʻi species have already become extinct, and the Kauaʻi species was last sighted in 1984. The bird in this drawing is the one that lived on Oʻahu. The yellow feathers of these birds were highly valued for making capes, helmets, leis, and other feathered ornaments. The enchanting song of the ʻōʻō was said to be the most beautiful of all the Hawaiian forest birds.

ʻAKIALOA

The ʻakialoa had the longest bill of any of Hawaiʻi's native forest birds. Its bill was very useful for probing into rotten tree bark for insects or worms or into long, curved flowers for nectar. Separate species of ʻakialoa inhabited the islands of Hawaiʻi, Oʻahu, Lānaʻi, and Kauaʻi. The bird in this drawing is the Kauaʻi ʻakialoa, which was last sighted in 1973.

ʻAKIALOA

ʻŌʻŌ

Patrick Ching '92

FLIGHTLESS BIRDS

Most of Hawai'i's flightless birds became extinct before the arrival of Captain Cook and are known to us only through fossils. We know that there were flightless geese, rails, and ibises that evolved with larger than normal legs and very small wings. In prehistoric times these birds could survive because there were no mammals in Hawai'i that hunted them. When the first people came to Hawai'i, they brought with them dogs and rats that made easy meals of the flightless birds. The people themselves also caught and ate the birds.

Today all of Hawai'i's flightless birds are gone. The last of our flightless birds, the Laysan rail, became extinct in 1944.

*Because the exact color patterns of the birds in this drawing are not known, you can make them any color you like.

FLIGHTLESS RAIL

FLIGHTLESS IBIS

FLIGHTLESS GOOSE

Patrick Ching '92 ©

ABOUT THE AUTHOR

Born and raised in Hawai'i, Patrick Ching possesses a deep-rooted love for the islands which is portrayed in his artwork and writing. His enthusiasm for wildlife, art and Hawaiiana is the driving force behind his work. He spends a good deal of time "in the field" working with Hawai'i's animals in their natural environments. Patrick devotes much of his energy toward educating the public about Hawaiian wildlife through slideshow productions, guided nature hikes, and multi-media artwork.

Copyright © 1992 by The Bess Press, Inc.
ALL RIGHTS RESERVED
Printed in the United States of America
ISBN: 1-880188-43-0

BOOKS TO READ

Ching, Patrick, *Exotic Animals in Hawai'i Coloring Book.* Honolulu: The Bess Press, 1988.
Ching, Patrick, *Native Animals of Hawai'i Coloring Book.* Honolulu: The Bess Press, 1988.
Shallenberger, Robert J., ed. *Hawai'i's Birds.* Honolulu: Hawaii Audubon Society, 1981.

ACKNOWLEDGMENTS

A special *Mahalo* goes out to the people and organizations who contributed their time and knowledge toward producing this book: Sheila Conant, Bruce Eilerts, Robert Pyle, the Bishop Museum, the Hawaii Audubon Society, the State Department of Land and Natural Resources, and the U.S. Fish and Wildlife Service.